Handyman Freedom Formula Volume #1: Mindset / Company Culture

How to thrive in the handyman industry and change the world while you are at it!

ALLEN LEE

Bob Goff, Lori Zimbardi

Allen Lee

HANDYMAN FREEDOM FORMULA VOLUME #1: MINDSET / COMPANY CULTURE

I dedicate this book to all my brothers at Celebrate Recovery who have shown me that change is possible! No matter what you struggle with in life, you can always make the choice to change. Changing takes consistent effort and involvement in making the next best decision!

About The Author

In August of 2016, Allen started a part-time business that quickly flourished. By January 1st, 2017, he was dedicating himself to it full-time, and through his dedication and strategic planning, he's built a company that thrives even without his constant presence.

Allen has now transitioned his focus to empowering others. He coaches fellow handymen, sharing the secrets to his success and helping them achieve the same level of freedom and scalability. While he still oversees the marketing, finances, and company culture of his own business, his passion lies in guiding others to build thriving handyman empires of their own.

Honest Lee Handyman Service LLC. team 2023

ALLEN LEE'S OTHER BOOKS

Handyman Pricing Handbook

Handyman Marketing Handbook

Handyman Sales Handbook

My Clubfoot Boots
(For my daughter)

To My Son
(For my son)

Contents

Foreword

Taking the leap to start a business on your own is one huge thing to be proud of. It takes a lot—a lot of resources, both financially as well as mentally! Allen does a fantastic job in this book discussing the mindset shifts necessary for a handyman business owner to take along this exciting journey. Allen not only shares what's needed but gives detailed examples of how he learned (the hard way) what needs to happen.

Just like in life, there are different stages in starting and growing a handyman business, and each stage requires a new set of skills. In this book, Allen tackles the mental skills needed to overcome the negativity we all face in life and how that relates to growing a business. He understands that the journey from dream to reality requires a shift in how you approach challenges, handle finances, and, most importantly, build a team.

Whether you're a seasoned handyman looking to expand or a complete newcomer eager to break ground, Allen's insights on fostering a positive company culture are invaluable. He reminds us that a business is more than just its bottom line; it's about the people who make it happen. Learn how to attract and retain top talent, build trust, and create an environment where everyone feels valued and empowered.

This book is your roadmap to building a thriving handyman business and creating a company you're proud to call your own. So, roll up your sleeves, embrace the mindset shift, and get ready to turn your vision into reality.

Allen's wisdom, along with his clear and engaging writing style make this a must-read for anyone aspiring to build a successful handyman business with a heart.

Enjoy the journey!

· Bob Goff

Chapter 1

Introduction to the Handyman Freedom Formula

Over the course of the last many years, I have talked with thousands of handyman business owners who had little to no clue about running the business side of a handyman business, let alone growing a business with employees. So I have been trying to figure out a way to deliver a clear-cut plan for handyman businesses worldwide that would be their road map to running their business and ultimately discovering the freedom they initially got involved in their handyman business to find!

One night, I woke from a dead sleep, and I had it! I quickly gct a piece of paper, scribbled down my thoughts, and went back to bed. In the morning I saw for the first time what would be the Handyman Freedom Formula.

The Handyman Freedom Formula is a road map, a detailed instruction manual that an individual can follow from thinking about starting this business to actually growing it with employees so the business can run without them!

This formula is structured as a Parthenon from ancient Greece. The formula is built on top of the Foundation of Mindset and Culture and eight distinct vertical pillars that are an important part of business: Pricing, Finances & Accounting, Marketing; Hiring, Intaking, Sales, Scheduling, Job Performance & Follow-up. The formula is topped off with the capstone of Systems and Processes. The systems and processes make all of the pillars run smoothly! This parthenon will create freedom for you, the freedom you desired when you started this business. If followed correctly and done with the accountability of others, the Handyman Freedom Formula will reap great rewards as it has me in my business.

This formula consists of all the steps I took to grow my handyman business which has provided me the freedom to focus on my family while the business runs itself! And this is only the beginning. As you follow the formula, your business will have exponential growth capability!

This formula consists of ten volumes and will teach you all you need to know to go from startup to freedom!

In Volume One (Mindset/Culture), you will discover how to have and maintain the correct mindset you need for growth. You will also learn how to create and sustain a stellar company culture that allows your employees to be trusted by the client and yourself!

In Volume Two (Pricing, Finance & Accounting), you will learn how to price jobs correctly and identify the many mistakes you and many others (including myself) have made that bled money out of their businesses. You will not only learn how to make more money but also how to retain more money in your business and pay yourself more money!

In Volume Three (Marketing), you will learn the simple strategies that most people overlook when discussing marketing their handyman business (Getting your business in front of people is easier than you think).

In Volume Four (Hiring), you will learn the ins and outs of hiring your first or 15th employee and the steps to make that happen successfully. Hiring is more than just finding someone who is good at their job.

In Volume Five (Intaking Clientele), we will dig into acquiring a CSR (Customer Service Relations Personnel) to intake all your clients. Believe me, it will make your job so much easier and your clients will thank you for it!

In Volume Six (Sales), you will learn an in-depth sales strategy to help you sell more jobs and spend less time quoting them. This creates more profit and way less headache!

In Volume Seven (Scheduling) you will learn how to profitably manage a schedule. You will learn concrete skills that focus on efficiency and sustainability when scheduling jobs and making the most out of each day.

In Volume Eight (Job Performance), you will take a deep dive into hiring your first or 20th technician. You will learn how to get yourself out of the field and find the right people for this very critical job. You will also learn how to properly pay your employees for maximum production and longevity of their employment with you. Plus, by doing all this, your employees will actually want to stick around!

In Volume Nine (Follow-up), you will discover the most valuable asset in your business: "The fortune is in the follow-up." Many handyman businesses are unknowingly leaving significant revenue on the table by not following up with their past clients. You will learn systems to make follow-up easier and the employees you need to make that possible.

In Volume Ten (Systems/Processes), we bring everything together for a grand finale! This volume covers every aspect of your business operations, from pricing and quoting to marketing, client intake, sales, scheduling, job performance, and follow-up. By implementing this formula, you can achieve the ultimate goal—FREEDOM from the day-to-day operations of your business.

Ultimately, the Handyman Freedom Formula is all about one thing—FREEDOM. And that's exactly what you can achieve if you commit to studying hard and working even harder!

Chapter 2

Mindset is everything

Back in 2021, I was invited to an all-men's super-early workout group, called F3, by one of my good friends. He invited me for about a year and a half before I actually went to my first workout. Every time he asked me, I always had the same excuses: #1, I don't wake up early, and #2, I don't work out. So there was no way I was going to join him. He asked me a few more times and I gave him the same old stories.

At some point, he wore me down, and I said yes. Even the night before my first workout, I gave him those same excuses I had used time and time again. But this time, something was different. I thought, "What's the worst that could happen? I go to one and then hate it and never go back. I can do that, just so this guy stops asking me."

I was so clueless about working out that I had to text my friend and ask him what to wear. I went to the store and got some cheap workout clothes (yeah, I didn't have any).

The next morning, I showed up at at 5 am to the workout. The rest of the day, I felt like my heart was going to pound out of my chest. I never knew my heart muscles could be so sore! But I survived, and I actually enjoyed, not necessarily the workout, but the fellowship with the other men.

On January 17th, 2023, I had my first workout with F3. Once a month, the workout group has what they call a "5k" day at their Wednesday workout. The members run a 5k before the sun even rises! I got up and went, not for the 5k, that sounded ridiculous, but to support one of my other friends who was celebrating his 100th post with F3 that morning. Lucky me, it just happened to be a 5k day so I knew I would have to run. I remember being so worried about the 5k because, after all, it is 3.1 miles and other than working out with this group the past six month, I had never run a day in my adult life. This 5k day was all about challenging yourself—you vs. you. It is timed, and the objective is to beat your time from your last 5k. Since I had never done a 5k, my expectations were very low. I honestly didn't think I could complete a 5k race.

At the beginning of the race, I started my stopwatch and planned to take a break and walk once I reached the half-mile mark. I hit the half-mile mark and thought I was done, but I challenged myself to keep running, even if it was at a slower pace until I hit at least the one-mile mark. I managed to reach one-mile and started walking for a little while. After a few minutes, I kept running and stopped to walk about three other times during that 5k.

The finish line was in sight, and just when I thought I was giving it my all, my friend, Rob (who originally invited me to F3) passed me up. I told him, "I know this 5k is you vs. you, but I can't let you beat me" (a little rivalry I guess). I quickly sprinted to the finish line, passing him up as I finished!

I finished that 5k with a time of just over 27 minutes, which I thought was pretty good, but what happened next is the crux of the story. Rob came up to me after the workout and told me, "You have a lot more in you because when you passed me, you were going about three gears higher than I was;

you have more to give!" When Rob told me this, it was like a burst of self-confidence I didn't know I needed! After that, my whole mentality shifted, not only in workouts but also in other aspects of life. I started to believe I had more in me than I thought.

A month later, when the 5k day came up again, I invited another friend to join me. The 5k day was so different from the last. It was the same course, the same rules, the get up before sunrise thing, but my mindset had completely changed! I went into the workout with confidence, knowing that I could do it and that I had more in me than I thought I did!

My friend and I ran that 5k and finished with a time of just over 25 minutes. I was amazed! I knocked two minutes off my time, and I was not in any better shape or knew any more about running than I did the previous month. The only difference was that I went into this 5k with the mentality that I could do this—I had a mentality shift!

So many people think they need to have all the right answers, all the right gear, and all the right figures before hopping into something and most of the time all they need is to go in with the right mindset!

The thing about mindset is that it often takes someone on the outside calling something out of us that we didn't know we had! I hope this book is that for you! I want to call you out to something greater than what you thought you had!

In this book, I will share many stories and hard truths that are geared toward showing you that you can do more than you think you can and I'll give you strategies to shift your mindset if you are stuck in a specific way of thinking.

Mindset is the very foundation of living an abundant life! If you simply believe in your potential, you will be amazed by what you can achieve. This book is a tool that will help set the foundation for your life and your handyman business!

The second part of mindset and how it relates to the growth of a business is equally as crucial. It's about instilling that mindset in your employees and your growing company, which we call **culture**. Culture is how you portray your values (mindset) in your business and give your employees, or future employees, a guidepost to follow to enact your core values into your business!

In the back half of this book, culture will be our focus, and I will give you insight into creating a great company culture so your business can thrive!

As you go through this book, I want you to remember two things. #1: Business growth follows personal growth. If you are not growing as a person, there is no way your business will grow. And #2: Look at what 98% of the population is doing, and do the exact opposite and you will be successful!

Chapter 3

Defining the Types
of Mindsets

Before digging into how my mindset has shifted over the years as I have grown my handyman business, I want to look at and define the types of mindsets out there. While we do this, I want you to look into yourself and pinpoint which mindsets you currently resemble. Also, a good thing to note is that you can have multiple mindsets at a time. You can even have a particular mindset in one area of your life and a different mindset for another area, so do some self-examination here! There are many different types of mindsets out there, but I want to highlight and define the most common:

- *Fixed mindset*: Individuals with a fixed mindset believe that their intelligence and abilities are set in stone and cannot be changed. This can lead to a fear of failure and a reluctance to try new things.
- *Growth mindset*: Individuals with a growth mindset believe that their intelligence and abilities are developed through hard work and learning. This can lead to a

willingness to take on challenges and believe they can achieve anything they set their minds to.

· *Abundance mindset*: Individuals with an abundance mindset believe there are enough resources in the world for everyone to succeed. This can lead to a sense of gratitude and a willingness to share with others.

· *Scarcity mindset*: Individuals with a scarcity mindset believe the world has limited resources and they need to compete with others to get what they want. This can lead to a sense of fear and a reluctance to take risks.

· *Positive mindset*: Individuals with a positive mindset focus on the good things in their lives and believe they can overcome challenges. This can lead to greater happiness and success.

· *Negative mindset*: Individuals with a negative mindset focus on the bad things in their lives and believe they cannot overcome challenges. This can lead to greater unhappiness and failure.

Let's hop into some definitions and attributes so we can see what each mindset looks like and how it portrays itself in business:

Chapter 4

Fixed Mindset

I used to always wonder when I would "grow up" and "become a man." For pretty much my first 25-30 years on this earth, I felt like I was an imposter—like when we used to put different book covers on our comic books so our parents thought we were studying when we weren't. Even as a man, I felt like a little boy trapped in someone else's body. I ultimately learned that I had a fixed mindset and thought I had to accomplish a specific thing or grow big muscles to be considered an adult.

A fixed mindset is a belief that no matter how much someone tries or learns, they are held back by their innate intelligence, abilities, and potential and that those are set in stone. This mindset can significantly impact someone's life, influencing their thoughts, behaviors, and outcomes.

Here are some common attributes of a Fixed Mindset. See if you can see yourself in any of these:

- Belief in innate talent and fixed abilities: Individuals with a fixed mindset believe their talents and abilities are predetermined and cannot improve through effort or practice. They tend to view their abilities as inherent traits rather than skills that can be developed.

- **Fear of failure and avoidance of challenges**: Fixed thinkers fear failure and avoid taking on challenging tasks or situations. Believing that failure reflects their innate abilities and intelligence, they may feel embarrassed or humiliated if they don't succeed.
- **Sensitivity to criticism and feedback**: Fixed thinkers are sensitive to criticism and feedback and may perceive it as a personal attack rather than an opportunity for growth. They become defensive or argumentative when faced with feedback, especially if it suggests they need to improve.
- **Comparison to others and tendency to give up easily**: Fixed thinkers compare themselves to others. This often leads to discouragement or intimidation when they see the success of others. Believing they lack the necessary skills to succeed,
- **Focus on outcomes rather than effort**: Individuals with a fixed mindset often focus on the outcomes of their actions rather than the effort they put in. They view their successes as a validation of their innate abilities, while their failures are seen as proof of their limitations.
- **Belief that effort is for those not smart enough**: Fixed thinkers view effort as a sign of weakness or inadequacy. Believing that they are not naturally talented enough if they have to work hard to achieve something.
- **Hiding flaws and avoiding risks**: Fixed thinkers try to hide their flaws or shortcomings to avoid being judged negatively. They may also avoid taking risks or trying new things, fearing they will fail and expose their limitations.
- **Difficulty accepting feedback and suggestions**: Individuals with a fixed mindset may have difficulty accepting feedback or suggestions, especially if it implies they need to change their approach or improve their skills. They

may view feedback as a criticism of their abilities rather than an opportunity for growth.

· **Preference for praise and validation**: Fixed thinkers seek praise and validation from others as a way to confirm their self-worth and abilities. They feel insecure if they do not receive positive reinforcement.

· **Difficulty learning from mistakes**: Fixed thinkers have difficulty learning from their mistakes, as they view them as a reflection of their innate limitations rather than opportunities for growth. They are reluctant to try new things for fear of making mistakes.

If you identify with some of these attributes, it's important to remember that any mindset can be changed. You can develop a growth mindset by embracing challenges, learning from mistakes, and seeking feedback. With effort and a positive attitude, you can overcome the limitations of a fixed mindset and achieve your full potential.

Wow, before we move on to the next mindset, I want to stop here and say that I can definitely see that at each point where I "felt" stuck in my business, I was actually struggling with a fixed mindset. Although I claimed that I wanted to grow, I was afraid of the challenges that growth would bring. I was also worried about what others would think of me if I failed, so I didn't do anything and falsely labeled it as "stuck in business" or "contentment." I needed to change my mindset if I wanted to achieve success in my business.

Chapter 5

Scarcity Mindset

My very first day of high school was one of the most embarrassing days of my young life. See, I grew up attending a private school for K - 8th grade and a large public school for high school. I saw high school as a time when I could "reinvent myself" and become one of the cool kids! I had decided, for some unknown reason, that I was going to be one of those cool-looking rocker kids. So I got myself all decked out in black pants and a black shirt. I even started wearing Vans skater shoes and finished my new look with a sweet wallet with a chain on it. Oh yeah, I was hot stuff!

On the first day of school, I didn't know anyone yet so I decided to grab some lunch and eat by myself when a senior approached me and asked, "Hey, do you skate?" I replied, "Nope," and he walked away.

This was an incredibly embarrassing experience, and you think it would have made me change a few things about my poser attitude, but that wouldn't come for another two years. I am sharing this story because I used to be afraid of people and what I thought they had that I lacked. This is a classic example of a scarcity mindset.

A Scarcity Mindset is a belief that there are limited resources and opportunities in the world, leading to a sense of fear, competition, and a focus on what one lacks rather than what they have. It is characterized by several attributes, including:

· **Fear of loss and competition**: Individuals with a scarcity mindset often experience fear of loss, believing that their resources or opportunities are dwindling. They see others' success as a threat to their own, leading to a competitive and envious mindset.
· **Focus on limitations and obstacles**: Scarcity thinkers tend to focus on the limitations and obstacles in their path, believing they inherently lack the resources or abilities to achieve their goals. This can lead to a sense of helplessness and self-doubt.
· **Self-protective and defensive behavior**: Scarcity thinkers often adopt a self-protective and defensive posture, fearing that others will take away what they have. They may become overly cautious, hesitant to share resources or collaborate with others, and quick to take offense.
· **Difficulty accepting criticism and feedback**: Scarcity thinkers often perceive criticism and feedback as personal attacks, believing it confirms their perceived limitations. They may become defensive, argumentative, or resistant to change.
· **Comparison to others and focus on outcomes**: Individuals with a scarcity mindset tend to compare themselves to others, focusing on external validation and outcomes rather than the process of learning and growth. This can lead to feelings of inadequacy and a loss of motivation.
· **Belief in fixed abilities and limitations**: Scarcity thinkers often believe that their abilities and talents are fixed and cannot be improved with effort or learning. This can

lead to a self-fulfilling prophecy, limiting their potential and hindering personal growth.

· **Difficulty delaying gratification and impulse control**: Scarcity thinkers may struggle with delayed gratification and impulse control as they feel a need to secure resources immediately due to the perceived scarcity. This can lead to short-term decisions that conflict with long-term goals.

· **Sense of entitlement and blame**: Individuals with a scarcity mindset may develop a sense of entitlement, expecting others to provide for them or feeling resentful when they don't receive what they believe they deserve. They also blame external factors for their setbacks rather than taking responsibility for their actions and choices.

· **Difficulty giving and receiving help**: Scarcity thinkers struggle to give or receive help, believing that they need to hoard their resources or that accepting help is a sign of weakness. This can lead to isolation and missed opportunities for collaboration and support.

· **Focus on scarcity rather than abundance**: Scarcity thinkers focus on what they lack, leading to a sense of deprivation and dissatisfaction. They overlook the abundance in their lives, focusing instead on the perceived limitations and obstacles.

If some of these attributes sound like you don't worry just yet, you can change anything you put work into. You can develop an abundance mindset by embracing a belief in limitless possibilities, focusing on gratitude, practicing generosity, and cultivating a sense of interconnectedness. With effort and a positive outlook, you can overcome the limitations of a scarcity mindset and create a more fulfilling and abundant life.

Chapter 6

Negative Mindset

In my high school, the first and last Friday of your Freshman year was known as "Freshman Friday." It's simply a day when the Juniors and Seniors initiate the Freshman into the new school. In other words, it was absolute chaos! Backpacks were stolen, students were dunked in trash cans, and one of my classmates was even duct taped to the basketball hoop pole! When I say chaos, I mean chaos.

I had made one friend by the first Friday, and we were trying to avoid the chaos and not become a piece of trash by walking around the back of the school. Just when we thought we were in the clear, my friend got smacked in the face with a flour balloon! Needless to say, I was out of there faster than you could say, "Bisquick." I ran all the way around the school and found refuge with a big group of freshmen in front of the gymnasium.

Looking back, it probably wasn't the smartest idea that we were all in one place, as we got hit with a few different concoctions of water balloons that day. However, between attacks, I got to know a few people around me, and we bonded over our shared misery. It was interesting that all these people were dressed like "rockers," just like me. However, on that day, we felt an overwhelming sense of hopelessness; we couldn't help but get sucked into a negative mindset. Our clothes and hair smelled like things they shouldn't have due to the grenades that had been launched at us, which only added to our misery.

A Negative Mindset is a way of thinking that focuses on the negative aspects of life and expects negative outcomes. It is characterized by several attributes, including:

- **Pessimism and hopelessness**: Individuals with a negative mindset tend to have a pessimistic outlook on life, believing that bad things will happen in the future. They focus on the obstacles and challenges ahead rather than the possibilities and opportunities.
- **Dwelling on mistakes and setbacks**: Negative thinkers often dwell on past mistakes and setbacks, ruminating on them and allowing them to shape their self-perception and future expectations. They may view themselves as incapable of success or unworthy of happiness.
- **Focus on problems and limitations**: Negative Thinkers tend to focus on problems rather than solutions, emphasizing their limitations and obstacles rather than their strengths and capabilities. They may see challenges as insurmountable and opportunities as unattainable.
- **Self-criticism and self-doubt**: Negative thinkers often engage in self-criticism, putting themselves down and doubting their abilities. They have low self-esteem and a negative self-image.
- **Fear of failure and avoidance of challenges**: Individuals with a negative mindset may experience a fear of failure, leading them to avoid challenges and opportunities that could lead to growth and success. They prioritize comfort and familiarity over potential rewards.
- **Blame and external focus of control**: Negative thinkers blame external factors, such as other people, circum-

stances, or bad luck, for their setbacks and failures. They relinquish control over their lives and attribute their outcomes to external forces.

· **Difficulty forgiving themselves and others**: Negative thinkers struggle to forgive themselves and others for mistakes or offenses. They may hold grudges and resentment, preventing them from moving forward and experiencing positive relationships.

· **Focus on the negative aspects of others**: Negative thinkers tend to focus on the flaws and shortcomings of others, engaging in critical judgment and gossip. They struggle to appreciate positive qualities and focus instead on perceived negativity.

· **Difficulty expressing gratitude and appreciation**: Individuals with a negative mindset may find it challenging to express gratitude and appreciation for the good things in their lives. They overlook positive aspects and focus instead on what they lack or desire.

· **Catastrophize and overgeneralize**: Negative thinkers have a tendency to catastrophize situations. They assume the worst possible outcomes and dwell on negative possibilities. They overgeneralize from specific experiences, believing that negative events reflect broader patterns of failure or misfortune.

It's important to note that everyone experiences negative thoughts and emotions from time to time. However, if these thoughts and emotions become pervasive and interfere with your daily life, it may indicate a more ingrained negative mindset. With effort and a positive outlook, you can overcome the limitations of a negative mindset and cultivate a more fulfilling and optimistic approach to life.

Chapter 7

Growth Mindset

Handymen all have that old Folgers can full of leftover screws and bolts and all kinds of parts from past jobs simply because "we know we might need them one day." We dare not let anyone throw them away because the day they get thrown away is the day we are going to need them. We know that every time we have been in a pinch on a job, we have gone to that trusty Folgers can and found just the right part or screw we needed to complete the job! We tend to have a growth mindset about those spare, used parts. It's an easy win; it just makes sense.

A Growth Mindset is a belief that one's intelligence, abilities, and potential can be developed through effort, learning, and persistence. This mindset is associated with a number of positive outcomes, including academic achievement, career success, and personal fulfillment.

Here are some of the key attributes of a Growth Mindset:

- Belief in the power of effort and learning: Individuals with a growth mindset believe their abilities can be improved through hard work and dedication. They embrace challenges as opportunities to learn and grow and not threats to their self-worth.

· **Persistence in the face of setbacks**: Growth thinkers are not easily discouraged by setbacks or failures. They view these as temporary obstacles rather than permanent roadblocks. They learn from their mistakes and use them as fuel for further growth.

· **Openness to feedback and criticism**: Growth thinkers are open to feedback and criticism, seeing it as an opportunity to identify areas for improvement. They are not afraid to admit when they are wrong and are willing to change their approach if necessary.

· **Focus on the process rather than the outcome**: Growth thinkers are focused on learning and growing rather than solely on the outcome. They are motivated by the intrinsic satisfaction of learning and improving rather than by external rewards or validation.

· **Willingness to take risks and step outside one's comfort zone**: Growth mindset individuals are not afraid to take risks and step outside their comfort zone. They see this as a necessary part of the learning process.

· **Belief that intelligence and abilities can be developed**: Growth mindset individuals believe that intelligence and abilities are not fixed but develop through effort and dedication. They view intelligence as a malleable trait rather than a fixed characteristic.

· **Focus on learning from others**: Growth thinkers are open to learning from others, recognizing that everyone has something to teach them. They are open to asking for help or advice when needed.

· **Willingness to embrace challenges and setbacks as opportunities for growth**: Growth thinkers view challenges and setbacks as opportunities to learn and grow. They use these experiences to identify areas for improvement and develop new strategies.

· **Belief in the power of self-reflection**: Growth mindset individuals are reflective learners who take the time to consider their progress and identify areas for improvement. They are not afraid to admit when they have made mistakes and are willing to make changes.

· **Belief in the power of positive self-talk**: Growth thinkers use positive self-talk to motivate themselves and encourage themselves to persevere in the face of challenges. They focus on their strengths and capabilities rather than their limitations.

If you want to develop a growth mindset, there are several things you can do:

· **Challenge your negative thoughts**: When you have a negative thought, ask yourself if it is true. Is there evidence to support it?

· **Focus on your successes**: Remind yourself of all the things you have accomplished in your life.

· **Set goals for yourself**: Having something to work towards can help you stay motivated and focused.

· **Learn from your mistakes**: Don't dwell on your failures. Instead, learn from them and use them as an opportunity to grow.

· **Be kind to yourself**: Everyone makes mistakes. Forgive yourself and move on.

Developing a growth mindset is an ongoing process that takes time and effort. However, the rewards are *well worth it.* A growth mindset can help you achieve your goals and lead a more fulfilling life.

Chapter 8

Abundance Mindset

We handy people must have a look or a smell because people who need something done that no one else wants to do always seem to find us.

One of my friends bought some property in the country a few years back, and the day he moved in, one of the neighbors called him and asked him if he would come over and shoot her horse because the horse was old and sick, and they couldn't afford the vet bill. My friend politely declined. He is up for almost anything, but this was a little out of his realm of expertise!

He thought he would never hear from that neighbor again, but two weeks later, he got another call from the same neighbor. She told my friend that the deed was done, but now she needed someone to bury her horse and asked my friend if he had an excavator.

Later that day, my handy friend went down the street in his excavator to bury the horse. Mind you, this is something he had never done before. He had a few questions that he asked himself: How big do I make the hole? Is it taboo to just push the horse in the hole, or is there some kind of respect that needs to be paid? Needless to say, he got busy digging the hole, and when it was time, he gingerly picked up the horse and set it in the hole. His concerns were realized when he found out the hole was not deep enough and the horse's feet stuck straight up. Not knowing what to do, he jokingly said, "You could put a table top on it and be comfortable!"

I think people find us handy people because we exude a "get it done" attitude! We tend to have an abundance mindset when we think about getting things done. Anything is possible; just do it, are some of our mantras!

An Abundance Mindset is a belief that there are enough resources and opportunities in the world for everyone to thrive. It is characterized by a sense of gratitude, generosity, and a belief in the power of collaboration. People with an abundance mindset tend to be optimistic, open-minded, and willing to take risks.

Here are some of the key attributes of an abundance mindset:

- **Belief in limitless possibilities**: Individuals with an abundance mindset believe there are endless possibilities for success and fulfillment in life. They are not limited by scarcity thinking and are open to exploring new opportunities.
- **Focus on gratitude**: Abundance thinkers are grateful for the abundance in their lives, big and small. They appreciate what they have and don't dwell on what they lack.
- **Willingness to share and collaborate**: Abundance thinkers are generous and willing to share their time, resources, and knowledge with others. They believe collaboration is key to success, and everyone has something to contribute.
- **Focus on personal growth**: Abundance thinkers are committed to continuous learning and personal growth.

They are always looking for ways to improve themselves and expand their horizons.

· **Belief in the power of win-win solutions**: Individuals with an abundance mindset believe that there are solutions that benefit everyone involved. They are not afraid to negotiate and compromise and always look for creative ways to create value for all parties.

· **Sense of optimism and hope**: Abundance thinkers are optimistic about the future and believe in the power of positive thinking. They are hopeful that they can achieve their goals and make a positive impact on the world.

· **Willingness to take risks**: Abundance thinkers are unafraid to take risks and step outside their comfort zones. They believe failure is a necessary part of the learning process and are willing to learn from their mistakes.

· **Focus on the present moment**: Individuals with an abundance mindset focus on enjoying the present moment and appreciate the abundance in their lives. They are not preoccupied with the past or worried about the future.

· **Belief that everyone has something to offer**: Abundance thinkers believe that everyone has something unique to contribute to the world. They are respectful of others and value their diverse perspectives.

· **Sense of interconnectedness**: Abundance thinkers believe that we are all connected and that our actions have a ripple effect on the world. They are committed to making a positive impact and creating a better world for all.

If you want to develop an abundance mindset, there are a number of things you can do:

· **Focus on the positive**: Pay attention to the good things in your life and express gratitude for them.

- **Practice giving and receiving**: Find opportunities to share your time, resources, and talents. Be open to receiving help and support from others as well.
- **Expand your comfort zone**: Challenge yourself to try new things and step outside your comfort zone.
- **Focus on your strengths**: Recognize your unique strengths and abilities and use them to positively impact the world.
- **Believe in possibilities**: Don't limit yourself by believing that there are insufficient resources or opportunities. Believe that there is enough for everyone to thrive.
- **Be open to collaboration**: Seek opportunities to collaborate with others and achieve shared goals.
- **Celebrate successes**: Take time to celebrate your successes, big and small.
- **Learn from setbacks**: View setbacks as learning opportunities and use them to grow and improve.
- **Spread positivity**: Be a source of positivity and encouragement for others.

Developing an abundance mindset takes time and effort, but the rewards are *well worth it.* It can help you achieve your goals, lead a more fulfilling life, and make a positive impact on the world.

Quite a few years ago, a client contacted me and inquired about the cost of a job they wanted done at their home. I gave them a rough estimate. They followed up with an unusual question, "How much would this job be if you did it in a tuxedo?" I couldn't help but chuckle, but this client was dead serious. They wanted me to do the job wearing a tuxedo! Obviously, I declined their request and, surprisingly, didn't get the job. I tell you this story because every abundant mindset has its limits, especially when the request goes against one's core values. It's like the story of my friend who wouldn't shoot his neighbor's horse. He might have done that for family, but not a stranger.

Chapter 9

Positive Mindset

My daughter was born with a couple of medical issues, one of which was Clubfeet. Usually, this condition is not too painful or a lengthy process to fix. But my daughter also had an underlying bone issue that caused her joints to be unusually stiff and crooked.

When my daughter turned one year old, we were at what we thought was the end of the clubfoot correction process. However, much to our surprise, the doctor came to us after performing the procedure and told my wife and me that my daughter's feet were being unruly, and he believed there was no hope for correction. He recommended removing her Achilles tendons completely, which worried us, and rightfully so. We asked the doctor what that would mean for her ability to walk and run, and he told us she would need braces to do so.

My wife and I decided to tell the doctor no to the procedure and seek a second opinion—can you say no to a doctor? We found out you could! We found a clubfoot specialist in another state, took a chance on hope for our daughter's future, and booked a consultation with this doctor.

We had a choice—would we choose the scarcity mindset or a positive mindset? We chose the positive mindset and took a huge leap, one that meant we had to live in another state for a month and a half while my daughter underwent many sets of casts and surgery on her feet. We are so happy we chose to focus on hope, as our daughter is now up and running with the rest! She even recently scored her first goal in soccer! What a delight it can be to choose the positive mindset!

A Positive Mindset is a way of thinking that focuses on the good aspects of life and expects positive outcomes. It is characterized by several attributes, including:

- **Optimism and hopefulness**: Individuals with a positive mindset tend to have a hopeful outlook on life, believing that good things will happen. They focus on the possibilities and opportunities ahead rather than dwelling on past mistakes or setbacks.
- **Resilience and adaptability**: Positive thinkers can bounce back from challenges and setbacks, viewing them as learning opportunities rather than insurmountable obstacles. They are adaptable and willing to adjust their plans when necessary.
- **Gratitude and appreciation**: Positive thinkers are grateful for the good things in their lives, big and small. They take time to appreciate their blessings and express gratitude to others.
- **Focus on solutions and possibilities**: Positive thinkers focus on finding solutions to problems rather than dwelling on them. They see possibilities and opportunities where others may see limitations and obstacles.
- **Self-acceptance and self-compassion**: Positive thinkers accept themselves for who they are, flaws and all. They practice self-compassion and treat themselves with kindness and understanding.
- **Focus on the present moment**: Positive thinkers focus on enjoying the present moment rather than dwelling on

the past or worrying about the future. They appreciate the good things in their lives right now.

- **Belief in personal power and agency**: Individuals with a positive mindset believe they have the power to create their own happiness and success. They take responsibility for their actions and choices.
- **A sense of purpose and meaning**: Positive thinkers have a sense of purpose and meaning in their lives. They feel connected to something larger than themselves and believe their actions positively impact the world.
- **A willingness to learn and grow**: Positive thinkers are always open to learning and growing. They embrace new challenges and experiences.
- **A sense of humor and playfulness**: Positive thinkers have a sense of humor and playfulness. They are able to find joy in the simple things in life.

If you want to develop a positive mindset, there are several things you can do:

- **Focus on the positive**: Pay attention to the good things in your life and express gratitude for them.
- **Practice positive self-talk**: Talk to yourself in a kind and supportive way.
- **Spend time with positive people**: Surround yourself with people who make you feel good and support your positive outlook.
- **Do things that make you happy**: Make time for activities that you enjoy and that bring you joy.
- **Take care of yourself**: Get enough sleep, eat healthy foods, and exercise regularly.
- **Learn from setbacks**: View setbacks as learning opportunities and use them to grow and improve.

- **Help others**: Helping others is a great way to boost your mood and feel good about yourself.
- **Practice mindfulness**: Mindfulness can help you to focus on the present moment and appreciate the good things in your life.

Developing a positive mindset takes time and effort, but the rewards are *well worth it*. A positive mindset can help you achieve your goals, lead a more fulfilling life, and make a positive impact on the world.

Chapter 10

Victim v. Champion Mentality

When I was nine years old, I woke up to something that I had never experienced before and had never experienced since. Our house was full of cops, my mom was frantically on the phone, and our neighbor was making us lunches for the day. I remember instant panic as I didn't know what was going on, but I could feel something had changed; something was different. That morning, our neighbor took us to our summer program at school, picked us up for the day, and took us to another neighbor's house, where our pastor was. Our pastor proceeded to tell me and my siblings that our dad had gone missing that morning, and they found out that he had taken his own life that day. This news shook my whole world; it was the moment when extreme worry and anxiety entered my life. Like everything, though, life went on, but things were very different; I came to cope with the loss of my dad through control. I felt like I needed to control everything and everyone in my life so that something like this never happened again. I remember not letting my mom leave the house without knowing where she was going and when she was coming home. Some of my attitude and coping mechanisms could be considered "normal" for a kid who just went through a traumatic life event like I had. Still, it's that "normal" that I want to talk about.

We are all born with a champion mentality, an extreme sense of optimism, a sense that anything is possible! But at some point in our lives, we meet hurt, and we develop a victim mentality, that little sinister angel that sits on our left shoulder. Whether it's someone in our kindergarten class who tells us that we are not as smart as them or we lose a loved one way before their time, these hurts become our identity.

We have to choose the champion mentality daily. In every single circumstance, there is something that a victim mentality says, and there's something that a champion mentality says about what is going on. The way that we overcome in life is by making the conscious evaluation of what the victim mentality is saying versus what the champion mentality is saying and then making a conscious choice to choose that champion mentality even though our past circumstances have implemented that victim mentality inside our minds. This is something that never goes away; we will always default to the victim mentality. Think of the last time someone cut you off in traffic; our brains go to an instant victim mentality (you're not alone; I go there too). The truth is that 98% of people choose the victim mentality, whereas 2% choose the champion mentality. We want to consciously do what the 2% does, but that is easier said than done.

You have a choice every single day, every single moment, on which mentality you're going to choose. The kicker is that it's a lot easier to choose the victim mentality because it's the place where we can be safe, it's the place where we can be comfortable, it's the place where we don't get called out for doing it wrong, but when we make that choice, to choose the champion mentality, we have the opportunity for greatness, the chance of success and also the opportunity for failure.

Adopting the champion mentality doesn't guarantee constant success. We will stumble and fall. But here's the difference: the champion mentality doesn't see failure as the end but as a stepping stone, a learning opportunity on the path to success.

Everyone struggles with a belief in themselves and their abilities, and ultimately, the cure for that is inside of yourself; you are the one who needs to make the decision to take a chance on yourself and see what happens. From my personal experience and talking to thousands of other people, I will tell you that you might just be surprised at what you can do if you choose the champion mentality!

Never expect anyone to do something for you that you are not willing to do for yourself!

Your past experiences have a significant impact on your current mindset. I believe that at some point in life, everyone needs to confront the hurt that they have, the pain that resurfaces when they're faced with hard decisions. Maybe it's a moment where one of your parents said something to you as a young child that damaged your self-confidence, or a moment where you tried really hard at something but failed and got made fun of. Everyone has a story of hardship that greatly influenced their outlook on life. I encourage you to face that hardship story head-on and spend time reflecting on it.

Identify the wrong or hurtful things that have been said or done to you and make the conscious decision to move past them. These experiences are real but do not need to hold you back from your potential. God made you, in his image, to do great things, but unfortunately, people have gotten in the way. Healing is found in forgiveness, and when you choose to move past those hurts and hardships, you'll discover untapped potential. Those hurts and pains were what held you back from realizing what you can truly do in this life!

The stress, anxiety, and control that I developed on that fateful day when I was nine years old has caused me much pain throughout my life. Feeling like I needed to control things to make it "normal" only gave me a false sense of control and ultimately isolated me from those around me. I eventually realized that trying to control people and my circumstances was the thing holding me back and leading me to make bad choices based on a false sense of reality. Once I started trusting others and surrounding myself with safe people who made safe decisions, I began to make better, clearer decisions because I wasn't so worried about controlling everything. I came to understand that God was in control and He had a great plan for my life, and I needed to trust that plan instead of trying to control everything.

Bad stuff happens in life, but that doesn't mean that life is bad or that we are bad. We all operate from a place of our own hurts and pains and, ultimately, our own victim mentalities. You have a choice to let those hurts that were done to you (that were done by hurt people) control you and dictate the choices and decisions you make, or you can click the restart button on your family legacy and make a conscious effort to choose something different—a champion mentality.

If you want more information on overcoming your past hurts, I would strongly recommend Celebrate Recovery. My family and I have been going to Celebrate Recovery since 2021, and it has greatly transformed our lives. It has helped us see our past hurts for what they are and develop tools to move past them in a healthy way!

Chapter 11

Life and Death

My wife and I have 3 kids, and she gave birth to each of them at home, completely natural, with no pain meds whatsoever. She's a complete rockstar! Childbirth is intense and something that a lot of people fear. Most see it as a medical emergency that requires the intervention of doctors, but fact is that people have been having babies at home for a very long time.

My wife has always wanted to tap into some of the lost connection with what our bodies were created to do, one of which is to give birth naturally. Birth is a natural experience and not a medical emergency.

As my wife prepared for each birth, I saw some strategic things that she did that were pivotal to making this deep connection with this natural experience.

The world is always telling us their side of the story. When it comes to childbirth, the world tells us that it is a scary and painful experience, with blame directed at the man for getting them into this predicament. However, my wife, being the rockstar that she is, did her own research and felt a longing in her life that spoke something different to her than what the world has said her whole life.

One thing that I think was pivotal to my wife's success in preparing and executing this natural experience was an affirmation board. For all three children, my wife created a board filled with positive affirmations of what she believed, what others have experienced, and ultimately truths about how her body was designed to go through this process, despite the world labeling it as difficult.

I want to connect my wife's story to yours. The world has been telling you certain things your whole life regarding starting and running a business: "That's hard." "Most people fail." "What if things don't work out? How will you provide for your family?" "Are you sure you're cut out for that?" The world has been filling you with thoughts on what you're about to do. It's time to do a little research, see if this is possible, and start surrounding yourself with people who speak life into you and the direction you want to go.

There is a hard truth that there is life and death in the power of the tongue, and this also applies to the words you speak to yourself in your mind. Let me ask you a question: When you wake up in the morning, do you tell yourself it will be a good day or a bad one? Choose your words wisely, for they hold the power to shape your reality and your future.

I am not saying that if you speak and think positively, everything will always work out in your favor because there will always be things that go wrong. But what I am saying is that if you speak and think negatively about your day and life, you are almost certainly taking away any possibility that anything could go right. How often have you heard people say to themselves, "This is the story of my life," when something goes wrong? This is a classic example of a victim mentality, just waiting for bad things to happen. Or when you accidentally spill some milk, you say, "Oh crap, I knew this day was going to suck." rather than, "Oh man, the milk spilled; let's get to cleaning." Or when traffic happens, do you act like the traffic is happening to you to ruin your day, or does it just happen to be rush hour?

Whatever you focus on, you empower. If you focus on pain or negativity, you will empower that, and that is what you will experience throughout life.

So I want to challenge you every day for the next week when you wake up, go to the mirror in your bathroom, and tell yourself (out loud) that today will be a good day, that's it, nothing fancy. Just do that for a week, and then send me an email letting me know how doing that little thing each day has helped your mindset. If you give that a shot, I can almost guarantee that you will see a big improvement in how you look at life. Sure, not everything will be fluffy bunnies and rainbows, but you can always find something positive if you are looking for it! So do this for a week and send me an email at handymanjourney@gmail.com.

Remember that you have the power to speak life or death into your life or your circumstance, so whatever it takes, I encourage you to find ways to speak positivity (life) into yourself and your business! Create an affirmation board, put sticky notes of things you are grateful for on your dash; whatever it is, do it. You only live once, so why go through life pounding on yourself? Think the best you can, and you will be surprised at how your perspective will shift.

Among all the naysayers, we are trying to find courage—courage to do what others think is crazy, the courage to start and run a business, something that the majority of people never do.

You need four things to find courage: a connection to a higher calling, a conviction that empowers you, a community that stands by you, and compassion to guide you.

Having a connection to a higher calling means that something greater than yourself is compelling you to do something; without a greater cause than yourself or simply to just make money, you will never stand up to the scrutiny that fear will put you through. So whether your reason for starting this business is a calling from God or a longing to leave a legacy for future generations, you need to cling to that higher calling because if you are just in it for the money, there will be an end eventually as your mindset just won't be able to keep up or you just simply won't be able to fill that hole in your heart that just keeps wanting more money.

Once you have a higher calling and have clung to it, you need a conviction that empowers you. Simply put, a conviction is a firmly held belief or opinion. For us crazy entrepreneurs, our convictions are usually based on wanting a better life for ourselves and future generations. This belief that entrepreneurship is the roadway to a better future has to be held firm, or the first client that yells at us or gets mad and says we are overcharging will send us back to our old job. One beautiful thing that entrepreneurship has to offer that I have greatly appreciated is the ability to not only create a better future for you and your loved ones but also the potential to change the world! One conviction I have always held is that it is extremely sad that some people are born into situations that give them no say. Unfortunately, this puts people, actual humans, in a position where they are mistreated and just have horrible lives. My business has helped change that for many people! As I will talk about later in this book, my company partners with a company to help free kids from the sex slave industry, and we also partner with an organization that helps rebuild homes that were damaged by wildfires. The amazing thing about business is that it has shown me that you can literally change the world—and that is amazing!

After you have a reason to fight this fight that's bigger than money and a conviction for something that will empower you, you need a community that stands by you through thick and thin. We have already talked about how the world influences our decisions and thoughts. We need a group of people who will speak a different word into our minds than what we hear from the naysayers. I love the quote by Jim Rohn: "You become the average of the five people you hang around." This is so massive because it says that if you want to be a millionaire, hang out with five millionaires, and you are bound to be the sixth. As you hang around people of different caliber, you will be pushed in your thinking and education. You will, by proximity, start gleaning information from these individuals that will help you achieve your goals.

Similarly, if you hang out with five deadbeats, you won't get much personal growth; in fact, it may lead you in the wrong direction. Choosing your social circle wisely is more impactful than you might realize. To connect with like-minded individuals, I highly recommend joining our free Facebook community, "The Handyman Journey Mastermind." Also, if you want to step it up, join our monthly coaching program, The Handyman Academy. You can get more information at www.Handyman-Journey.com/coaching

You have that calling, conviction, and community; now, you need compassion. Compassion for why you started this thing in the first place, compassion for yourself, your community, and most of all, compassion for the people you serve. Many people in this world have strong convictions and surround themselves with people who hold those same convictions, but at the end of the day, they are complete jerks because they have no compassion.

Compassion says we are here on this mission to care for people, not just make our voices heard but also for people along the way. Caring for people also includes people who don't think like you; just because someone doesn't believe what you believe or have the same convictions as you, that doesn't make them a bad person. Their beliefs may be bad, but are they a bad person? I'd argue that most people have good intentions; we have different ways of looking at things. Don't get me wrong; there are people out there with ill intent, but most of us, when we get down to it, just want to help. As we are out there performing our mission, we need to constantly ask ourselves how we can be compassionate to those around us.

One part of choosing a champion mentality is understanding that we all operate out of our default, the victim mentality. That means when someone cuts us off in traffic or does something that seems rude, we need to understand that they are operating out of a place of hurt. Sometimes the most compassionate thing we can do for that person is show them love. There is a time for corrective words, but that time is short and far between. I love the saying by Francis of Assisi, "Preach the gospel at all times and if necessary, use words." What this means is our actions speak louder than our words. Let us be kind to people as they are going through some of their own pains that we have no clue about.

These four key components of courage will propel you on this journey. Still, it's a daily battle because, for every step in the positive direction we make, the world is going to try all the harder to suck us back into the victim's way of thinking; we must always be vigilant about where our minds are at!

I was recently at an education store with my family. While looking around, I came across some posters that tied in very nicely to this topic of mindset; two posters stood out to me, one about thoughts and one about affirmations. As we have already discussed, the world has been filling our minds with negative thoughts regarding this leap, so we must produce every weapon we can to fight against that. These two posters I came across are designed to go on a school wall, which is great. They teach young kids to think about their thoughts before their thoughts just mindlessly run them. So, these posters may seem a little childish, but at the end of the day, we all need to be reminded of these truths. If it will help you, get some posters and put them up in the room of your house where you work, your office, or even in the cab of your work truck; get these words in your head constantly and watch your mind-set shift. I have recreated the posters here to better fit our discussion.

Mindset Matters

Instead of..   Try thinking...

Instead of..		Try thinking...
"I failed and I embarrassed myself."	→	"I'm proud that I even tried, that took courage."
"I can't make this work."	→	"I can do this and I will do my best."
"I made a mistake."	→	"I can learn from this."
"This is too hard."	→	"If I keep practicing, it will get easier."
"They are better at it than I am."	→	"What can I learn from them?"

The Handyman Journey

MINDFUL AFFIRMATIONS

POSITIVE THOUGHTS TO START YOUR DAY

I GOT THIS

I WILL SHOW MYSELF COMPASSION

I AM PRESENT IN THIS MOMENT

I WILL FOCUS ON WHAT BRINGS ME JOY

I CHOOSE TO FOCUS ON IMPROVING MYSELF TODAY

I WELCOME TODAY'S OPPORTUNITIES

I ACCEPT MY THOUGHTS AND FEELINGS

I AM GRATEFUL FOR THE ABILITIES I HAVE

I AM GRATEFUL FOR WHO I AM

Let's hop into some mindset shifts that I have gone through at different stages of my business journey, may my mistakes and shortcomings be your golden education!

Chapter 12

Mindset Shifts in the Growth of a Handyman Business

As a child, I would spend hours playing certain video games. Although the normal game levels were not very challenging, the boss level always got me. I would get stuck on a boss level for hours on end only to realize that beating it required me to do completely different things than I had done in the standard levels. The boss levels were designed in a way that calls you to a greater place in your gaming. It seemed as though the game developers had designed the boss level to be much harder than the previous standard levels. This made me realize I would need to improve my skills to beat the rest of the game. Or perhaps the game developers were jerks and just wanted to see kids waste their time.

Since 2016, there have been a few key moments in my business that, just like that boss level, I had to change my way of thinking and look at the challenges in a different way! I had to shift my mentality to overcome these obstacles, and although my business is not perfect and I am not an expert, I have been through the trials of staying up late at night trying to beat the boss levels of my business!

Along the way, I have learned a few hacks that have helped me. I have also learned to identify when I am struggling and need to call in support. I will share those key moments and mindset shifts I have had to make in my business. My guess is that you will encounter the same boss levels as I have.

Each shift has several levels and sub-mentalities that I will explore in detail in the following chapters. By understanding these shifts, my hope is that you will better identify where you are in your business and possibly glean some insight into how I dealt with them and how you can, too.

- Startup Mindset
    - You can do it mindset
    - You need others mindset (you can't do it alone)
- Business Mindset
    - Pricing mindset
    - Marketing mindset
    - Sales mindset
- Hiring Mindset
    - Systems mindset
    - Trust mindset
    - Delegating mindset (no more codependency)
- Collaboration Mindset
    - We are all human mindset
    - Drop the ego, it's all about helping others
    - Gain more by giving away Mindset

Chapter 13

Startup Mindset

Picture a baby first learning to walk; the child stands up, attempts their first steps, and then falls flat on their face. What do you say to the child? "You're no good at this; you should quit now before you make a fool of yourself!" No! We would never say that to a child first learning to walk; that would be messed up.

Often, when we are learning new skills, we talk to ourselves in a way that hurts our learning abilities and, most of all, our mindset. The first thing you need to know about a startup mindset is to give yourself some grace. A little secret: You *are* going to fall flat on your face! What matters most is whether you stand back up or not!

A Startup Mindset is a unique approach to business that prioritizes agility, learning, and adaptation.

Here are some key aspects:

- **Action orientation:** It's about getting things done and testing ideas quickly. Don't get bogged down in overplanning; get your service out there and gather feedback. *Done is better than good. Sure, good is the goal, but it can't be good if it never gets done.*

- **Embrace risk:** There's inherent uncertainty in starting a business. *As a business startup, you have to realize that there are no failures, only learning experiences!*
- **Resourcefulness:** Bootstrapping and making the most of what you have is crucial. Startups often need to be scrappy and find creative solutions with limited resources. Sometimes, this means strapping a ladder to the top of your Prius and getting busy—whatever it takes!
- **Customer focus:** Understanding your target audience and their needs is paramount. A startup mindset prioritizes getting your service in front of customers early and adjusting things based on their feedback.
- **Innovation and creativity:** Thinking outside the box and challenging the status quo are essential. *The key to success is looking at what 98% of people are doing and do the exact opposite!*
- **Lifelong learning:** Things are ever-evolving. You must embrace continuous learning and adaptation to new technologies and market trends.

A startup mindset is about being flexible, resilient, and passionate about your idea. It's about calculated risks, learning from mistakes, and iterating your way to success.

When I first started my business, I was flooded with various thoughts. One was, "Who is going to trust me in their home? I'm just me. Can I really do this?" All I can say is you need to have faith in yourself first. You have to believe that you have been given the abilities you have for a specific reason and stand firm in that!

The second thought that quickly came to my mind after I started my handyman business was a strong feeling of loneliness. Prior to becoming a handyman, I worked as an automotive technician, where I was used to working with other people every day. There was always someone in the bay next to me that I could ask questions or share ideas. However, as a handyman, I realized that I was working alone most of the time. I went searching for groups or communities, but back in 2016, there weren't many. So, I started a Facebook group called "The Handyman Journey Mastermind." It was extremely helpful not just for me but for many others as well.

Even now, as of the writing of this book in 2024, this group has over 12,000 other handymen who use it as a great resource to not only combat the loneliness factor that comes with this profession, but it is also an amazing resource for knowledge and a place to bounce off ideas. I realized early on that trying to do this business alone can lead to burnout or finding yourself in tricky situations with no clue how to get out.

I remember a time when I was brand new in the handyman business and had just started the Handyman Journey Facebook group. I was installing a dog door panel in a sliding glass door. It started off as a pleasant job and everything was going well, until it wasn't. It was a beautiful day and the family I was working for was enjoying a nice day in their backyard, eating lunch on their patio table while I worked nearby.

I was almost done with the installation, and the clients loved it. The last thing left was to install the toe kick sliding glass door lock. I needed to install a lock on the ground that would slide a bolt through the frame of the sliding glass door to lock it when shut. I marked out where I needed to drill the hole into the sliding glass door, and you can probably imagine what happened next.

As I drilled, I must have nicked the edge of the glass pane. The sliding glass door shattered right over my head and right in front of the clients, who were enjoying a nice picnic lunch. I instantly looked up at the clients with an "oh crap" look on my face, and they stared back with a very similar expression! I didn't know what to do, and various questions came to my mind—questions I didn't have the immediate answers to like: How do I get this fixed?

After all, it was a house built in the 1970s, and I didn't think I could go to Home Depot and easily buy a new sliding glass door panel. I was also unsure about how I would discuss the price with the clients. In a moment of desperation, I turned to "The Handyman Journey Mastermind" group on Facebook, and like an answered prayer, many people from around the world shared their thoughts, opinions, and prayers (I needed those!).

Long story long, I found a local glass shop (which was recommended by a member of the Facebook group!), and I didn't charge the client for the job. It was a costly learning experience but not a failure! It's a story that I will never forget. When push comes to shove, the more people you have in your corner of the ring, the better! Surround yourself with people who will encourage you and also give you the hard truth when you need it.

There are two types of people in this world, there are consumers and producers and by making the conscious choice to start up your own business you are by default choosing to become a producer. The fact is that producers think wildly different that consumers. You have presumably been a consumer your whole life up until this point, there will be things that need to change and the majority of those changes need to take place in your mindset. Simply put, if you don't start thinking like a producer your business will not last long.

A **consumer** focuses on immediate gratification and acquiring goods or services to fulfill needs or wants. They prioritize spending money on experiences or possessions that provide short-term enjoyment. While a **Producer** focuses on creating value and contributing to the world. They prioritize investing their time, energy, and resources into building something, whether it's a product, service, skill, or knowledge.

A consumer values convenience, pleasure, and immediate satisfaction. They often base their decisions on the perceived value they get for the price they pay. While a producer values long-term growth, impact, and contribution. They are willing to put in effort and potentially delay gratification to achieve a bigger goal.

A consumer spends money on acquiring finished goods and services. While a producer invests money in tools, resources, and learning to create something of value.

Ultimately a consumer often has a scarcity mentality, focusing on what they lack and what they need to acquire. While a producer has an abundance mentality, believing in their ability to create and contribute. They focus on possibilities and solutions. You need to consciously choose, everyday, to put that abundance mindset on because you are no longer just a consumer, you are a producer!

You can do this. Believe in yourself, take a chance, and surround yourself with supportive people who want to help you succeed!

Chapter 14

Business Pricing Mindset

In December 2016, when I was still working part-time, a client found me on Yelp and contacted me for a simple gutter cleaning job. I visited their house one evening (in the dark) after my day job to give them an estimate and hopefully do the work.

The client showed me the gutters that needed cleaning and a gutter downspout in the ground drain connector that needed to be reinstalled. I quoted a price of $100 to do the job. The client said, "So your $50 an hour?" to which I said, "Yes." So we agreed, and I got busy!

After completing the job, I called the client out to show her my work, and she asked for the final bill. I reminded her that we agreed on a flat fee of $100. She insisted that I had only been there for an hour and a half and that I should be paid accordingly. I instantly knew what she was getting at, and I was internally a little angry. I realized that charging by the hour was inefficient and could work against me. She paid me S75.00 and I never worked for that client again. It was a hard lesson learned that day.

I often hear handymen express guilt when it comes to pricing their services. They feel guilty for charging customers a certain amount simply because, as a handyman, they would never pay someone that much to do the same job. They would simply just do it themselves.

Here are a few mindset shifts to help you understand the value of your services and charge accordingly. I have learned these shifts throughout the years and want to pass them along to you.

- **You are not your ideal client**: As a handyman, you are not and will never be your ideal client. As handymen, we are people who get stuff done; if we don't know how to do it, we figure it out, and we don't hire people. Our ideal clients are not like us. Understanding our client's mindset and needs is essential to provide them with the best service possible. Our ideal clients prefer to hire professionals because they might not have the skills, time, or desire to do the work themselves. That is why we are here.
- **Focus on the value you provide**: Not just the time spent. Consider the convenience, expertise, problem-solving, and saved time you offer to the customer. If you charge by the hour, the quicker you work, the less money you make. I recommend charging by the job, not by the hour. The more you learn, the more efficient you become and the more value you provide—and ultimately, the more money you make.
- **Price based on project complexity and expertise needed**: Not just a flat hourly rate. Complex projects with specialized skills deserve a higher price point.
- **Offer tiered pricing or packages**: By providing different service levels, you can make it easier for your clients to choose the option that best suits their needs and budget.

If the client has a budget, you can often work with them to fit the work they need to be done into their budget. For instance, if they need ten tasks done that will cost $1000, but they only have a budget of $800, you can suggest breaking the project into two parts: five projects now and five next month or eight projects now and two later. This approach can build trust and friendship with your clients because it shows that you care about their needs while also taking care of your own needs. If this is an ideal client, then they will be willing to work with you because they respect your needs and understand that it is a professional relationship.

Confidence and profitability:

· **Don't undersell yourself**: Know your worth and the value you offer. Research your local market and competitors, but **don't be afraid to charge a fair price** that ensures your business is profitable. One book I recommend on this subject is a book we wrote a few years back, *the Handyman Pricing Handbook*. In this book, we go in-depth on figuring out what your rates need to be as a handyman and how to weigh that against various other demographic values to land at a reasonable price that ensures you are fair but also make a profit on every job.

· **Be transparent about your pricing structure**: Clearly communicate hourly rates, minimum charges, travel fees, and materials costs. Avoid hidden fees or surprises. There are many different thoughts on this, but we itemize our estimates, laying out what each project will cost as well as any other miscellaneous fees or mileage charges that we include on the estimate. We are open to discussing any of these charges with our clients because, at the end of the day, we need to charge what we need to charge. If a client is not okay with a $5 mileage charge, then they are not our ideal client and it is best to find that out early in the process rather than during the job. We go in-depth into these additional charges in the *Handyman Pricing Handbook* as well.

· **Be confident in justifying your prices**: Be prepared to explain the value you provide and the expertise you bring to the table. I have found confidence in explaining my prices by making it about the client rather than about me. For instance, I often tell my clients that our two main goals are to do the best job and provide the best service possible, which requires a certain level of investment. It costs money to have the right tools, hire professional individuals who can be trusted in your home, and so on. The more we can make things about the people we serve, the more we create a deeper connection and trust, and the more they will connect with our mission.

Upselling and added value:

· **Charging for additional items**: It is important to consider your expenses and charge accordingly. Don't be afraid to charge for things like dump fees, one-time-use supplies, gas, etc.
· **Package services strategically**: Bundle complementary services to offer a discounted rate and encourage customers to choose larger projects. For instance, you could offer a "spring cleaning" package, which includes gutter and dryer vent cleaning.
· **Focus on customer satisfaction**: It's all about the customer, so focus on them. By delivering exceptional service and exceeding expectations, you can build trust and encourage repeat business, which is ultimately more profitable.

Mindset shifts:

- Think like a business owner, not an employee: Understand your costs and overhead and factor them into your pricing. As an employee, making $30 per hour may seem great, but it doesn't go very far when you have to pay bills as a business owner.
- Value your time and expertise: *Don't be afraid to charge what you're worth because if you don't look out for yourself, no one will.* Seriously—read that again and again and again!
- Focus on long-term sustainability: Prioritize building a loyal customer base and a positive reputation over maximizing short-term profits through low prices.

Remember: Pricing is just one aspect of your business. By combining a **value-based approach, confidence in your worth, and a focus on customer satisfaction**, you can develop a successful pricing strategy for your handyman business.

Chapter 15

Business Marketing Mindset

One evening in 2016, I was called out to a client's house to look at some work she needed done. One of the jobs she needed was cleaning her chimney (I had only ever cleaned one chimney in my life). I looked at it and told her I would return the following Saturday to clean it out (I didn't feel like getting on her roof at night, in the dark).

That Saturday, I cleaned out her chimney, and I was super proud of myself. I had looked up a how-to on YouTube and made myself a cool contraption. It was a piece of plywood with a vacuum attachment on it. I put it up to the fireplace opening and turned on the vacuum while I cleaned the chimney from the roof. It worked great at sucking up all the soot as I cleaned. I'm only sharing this story because it came to my mind, and I thought it was a good solution! The chimney cleaning has nothing to do with marketing, but how the client found me does.

I was curious about how the client found me, so I asked her. She replied that she found me on Yelp which surprised me because Yelp isn't a popular platform among tradespeople. When

I first started up my handyman business I did two things in marketing that I still do today: I hired Handyman Marketing Pros to build my website and handle my SEO, and I paid Yelp $300 per month to advertise.

Since the client found me on Yelp, I was intrigued, so I asked her more about it. She told me that she only uses Yelp to find tradespeople when she needs work done. She went on to leave me a review on Yelp, and I still have her as a client to this day.

Hearing this client's story of how she only uses Yelp points us to our first mentality shift: **That we shouldn't always listen to hearsay**. While there are many handymen who are adamantly opposed to Yelp and have some good stories of how Yelp did them wrong, I have built my business on Yelp and have had positive experiences. When people give you advice, take what works and leave what doesn't. You have to test what works for you and your business because your business is unlike anyone else's.

It is also important to have patience when it comes to marketing. On average, it takes at least 90 days for marketing efforts to pay off. If you have been marketing for a month, and it seems like you're not gaining any traction, keep it up. Marketing is a mathematical game: you invest x amount, and you get x amount of calls. That calculation is different for every business.

Once you have been marketing for a while and you start building traction, it is like a snowball effect. The longer you keep going, the bigger the snowball gets. Your brand and connection with the community keep growing. I also want to let you know about our *Handyman Marketing Handbook* that I wrote a few years back. It goes in-depth on Handyman marketing and the do's and don'ts associated with it.

A **Proactive and Value-Driven Mindset** is crucial for a handyman when marketing your business. Here are some key aspects:

Don't think of your business as "selling" but think of it as "helping":

- View yourself as a **problem solver** who fulfills customer needs, not just someone selling a service. I love the saying, "People don't care how much you know until they know how much you care!" This is so true, especially in the handyman space!
- **Just like pricing, you want to focus on the value you bring** to the client and, ultimately, the problems that you solve.

Embrace community and relationships:

- Recognize the **power of word-of-mouth marketing**. Build trust and encourage positive recommendations through exceptional service. Studies show that each person knows about 600 people, so by creating a happy client, you are increasing your chances of them telling one or more of the 600 people they know about you!
- **Network with local businesses and organizations** like realtors, property managers, and neighborhood associations. Don't be afraid to get out there and network. The more you are out in your community, the more people will talk about you and the work you do!

Become a local brand and thought leader:

- **Establish yourself as a trusted expert** by sharing helpful content like DIY tips for solving common repair challenges through blog posts, videos, or social media. One huge thing I have coached many handymen on is simply posting daily on Facebook and Instagram. It may seem like an unimportant thing to do, but the consistency of being active online every day pays big as time goes on! Posting funny questions can help engagement as people love responding to those!

· **Focus on local marketing efforts.** If you haven't yet, claim your Google My Business listing and create all the free online accounts you can. It's important to be wherever your ideal clients are!

Embrace continuous learning and adaptation:

· **Stay informed about industry trends and customer behavior online.** Go to www.handymanmarketingpros.com and download their free marketing guide—you can thank me later!

· **Track your marketing efforts.** Always ask clients how they found you, and adapt your strategies based on data and feedback to improve your overall effectiveness.

· **Invest in learning new marketing skills** and explore cost-effective solutions to reach your target audience. One thing that is changing the game for marketing is AI. You can now use AI for so many amazing things, including creating your content for social media!

We recently put together a free training on AI and marketing that we want to give readers of this book for free. Go to https://bit.ly/HandymanMarketing to get access now.

Overall, a successful marketing mindset for a handyman involves:

· Prioritizing customer needs and satisfaction.

- Proactively building trust and positive relationships within the community.
- Embracing innovation and continuous learning to stay ahead of the curve.
- Being strategic and data-driven in your marketing efforts.

Adopting a **proactive, value-driven, and community-focused mindset** can effectively promote your business, attract new customers, and build a successful long-term brand.

Chapter 16

Business Sales Mindset

In 2017, a client called me (they found me on Yelp—again), needing some drywall patches done after a plumber had come through and fixed some pipes. The moment he called; I quickly drove the 30 minutes to his home to take a look. I got there to find out he had nine holes cut in various places throughout his home. As we walked through the home, he asked me what it would cost. I instantly got nervous and threw out a price of $250 (yikes). He quickly accepted the bid. As we continued to walk through and look at the holes, which were about 2' x 2' in size, he asked me if I would paint them as well. I said, "Sure," and told him that would be an additional $50 (I cringe just telling this story!). He agreed to the job, and I naively agreed as well.

I came back a week later to start the job. The first day, I patched all the holes and retextured everything, then came back the following day to paint everything. He "had" the paint, and what he meant by "had" was old, leftover paint in jars from when they painted the house seven years prior.

We spent the next hour looking through all his jars in the garage to find the right colors because, of course, every room was a different color. We finally found the right colors, but sure enough, all the paint had solidified and was unusable. I had to get new paint at the local hardware store.

By the end of the day, I had painted all the patches. The client insisted on waiting to pay me until the paint dried and he could see the finished results. I headed home, my second day on this job, with no money in hand.

The next morning, the client called, saying the texture looked horrible and that I needed to come fix it. That texture story is a story for another time. Long story short, after five trips to this guy's house and a lot of money spent learning valuable lessons, I got the job done and received my $300. I chalked this job up to a learning experience. The biggest lesson I learned was to make sure I had proper pricing. The second biggest was a crash course in sales. I now know that I don't need to drive out to every client's house the moment they call.

There is value in slowing down, getting pictures, and giving a rough ballpark estimate over the phone. A few things happened during this client's interaction that set me up for failure. #1: I went to the client's home blind—not knowing what was needed or expected. #2: I didn't give myself enough time to think through the job before I gave a price.

When we feel pressured to provide a quote on the spot, whether that pressure comes from the client or ourselves, we tend to deeply undercut our value and throw out a low number in the spirit of not offending or simply getting the job. I have learned it is better not to get a job than to do it for less than it's worth.

The key to sales is to not be a greasy car salesman but be a trusted advisor! Here are a few other key mindsets I have learned about sales:

- **Peel the onion by focusing on understanding customer needs:** Actively listen to their challenges and frustrations, not just their desired services. Someone may call wanting a bath faucet replacement. Unless you ask deeper questions, you will never understand why they want it replaced. It could be dripping constantly and keeping them up at night. Once you know why, you are not just replacing their faucet, but you are selling them a solution to a better night's sleep!
- **Become a problem solver:** Offer solutions that address their specific needs and demonstrate your expertise in providing the best outcome. Don't be afraid to solve a customer's problem for free if it's a simple fix. I have been on many estimates where one of the things a client would like fixed is a closet door that is off track, and I can reset it right then and there. That is the kind of service that turns a person into a customer!
- **Focus on value, not just price:** Highlight the benefits beyond the hourly rate, such as convenience, time saved, peace of mind, and high-quality results.

Embrace Transparency and Trust:

- **Set realistic expectations:** Explain timelines, potential challenges, and what's included in the service. One approach I find effective is to ask the client, "If we get out there and realize that this job will take longer or cost more than we quoted you because we found something we didn't see, would it be ok if we called time out and had a conversation about what the job will look like moving forward?" Most clients love this approach and welcome this discussion. If you are interested in more of our sales process and how you can create one for your business, I recommend checking out one of our other books called *Handyman Sales Handbook.*

· **Maintain ethical practices:** Be honest about your capabilities and limitations and prioritize customer satisfaction. A very important attribute that we hold as one of our core values is that we will always do the right thing even if we end up losing money. Our clients appreciate this level of dedication.

Customer-centricity is Key:

· **Prioritize customer satisfaction in every interaction:** Go the extra mile to deliver exceptional service and build trust for repeat business and positive word-of-mouth recommendations.

· **Actively seek feedback:** Request feedback after completing a project and continuously look for ways to improve your services and communication. If a client leaves you a bad review, take this opportunity to learn from it. Rarely do you get the chance for a client to openly tell you what they would like improved about your business. A negative review is a clear sign that a system in your business needs improving.

· **Maintain professional demeanor:** Be punctual, courteous, and responsive to customer inquiries and concerns. Never badmouth or argue with a client; these actions will only end up weakening your reputation!

Embrace Continuous Learning:

· **Stay updated on industry trends and best practices:** Attend workshops, read relevant articles, and participate in online communities to improve your skills and knowledge.

· **Refine your sales pitch:** Practice your communication style, refine your responses to common objections, and adapt your approach based on customer interactions.
· **Learn from every interaction:** Analyze every sales experience, both successful and unsuccessful, to identify areas for improvement.

Adopting a **customer-centric, problem-solving, and transparent approach**, can build trust, effectively communicate their value, and close deals successfully. This mindset, continuous learning, and professional conduct will contribute to a thriving handyman business.

Chapter 17

Hiring Mindset

When I hired my first handyman employee, I had the worst collection of bad mindsets when it came to hiring. I was controlling, untrusting, and very codependent. Over time, I realized my mistakes, and I have come a long way on this journey learning from my ups and downs.

So, your handyman business is thriving. You're juggling a million tasks, but the workload is becoming overwhelming. It's time to consider hiring your first employee. This exciting step marks a significant shift from the solopreneur lifestyle. However, before diving headfirst into resumes and conducting interviews, a crucial first step is cultivating the right **hiring mindset** and becoming aware of any negative mindsets you may have.

Letting Go of Control: Embracing Collaboration

Letting go of complete control can be a daunting task, especially for most people and solopreneurs who are used to wearing many hats.

Hiring an employee requires a mindset shift towards delegation, a few benefits of this are:

- **Focus on Your Strengths:** Identify your core business skills and delegate tasks that drain your time or energy (things that you suck at). Focus on what you do best while your employee tackles other areas. For example, I was terrible at answering the phone and returning calls, which was hurting my business's reputation. So, my first hire was someone to take on these tasks. This allowed me to focus on my core business skills while ensuring that my clients were well taken care of.
- **Trust Breeds Growth:** Giving your employees ownership of tasks fosters learning and initiative. This not only benefits your business but also helps your employees develop professionally. Showing your employees that you trust their decisions will empower them to make better decisions and ultimately make decisions that you would make even when you aren't around.
- **Building a Team:** You can't do it all alone. You need to shift your mindset from doing it all to delegating. As you delegate, your business will be able to serve your clients in a more impactful way than you ever could have on your own.

From Taskmaster to Leader.

Hiring your first employee requires a transition from solo operator to leader. This new role demands a focus on:

- **Clear Communication:** I have coached thousands of business owners on the need to create and communicate company core values. These values are the lifeblood that spurs you and your employees on to make wise decisions. Open communication fosters trust and a healthy working relationship.
- **Delegation with Direction:** Don't just delegate tasks; provide clear instructions, support, and resources to ensure

success. This is where systems and processes come into play. One book that was massive in my learning was "The E-myth Revisited" by Michael Gerber. I highly recommend you pick that book up.

· **Mentorship and Feedback:** Offer guidance and constructive feedback to help your employee learn and grow within their role.

Hire for personality, not skill; *You can't train personality, but you can train skill.*

Technical skills are essential, but a successful hire requires considering a broader scope:

· **Cultural Fit:** Look for someone who aligns with your company culture and values. This creates a cohesive and positive work environment. Before inviting candidates for an interview, it's important to have a clear idea of your ideal employee. This includes their communication style, problem-solving skills and overall demeanor. These qualities should align with your company's core values. Once you have a clear understanding of what you are looking for, finding the right employee will be a lot easier.

· **Learning Agility:** The ability to adapt and learn new skills is crucial in a dynamic small business environment.

· **Positive Attitude:** A positive and enthusiastic employee can significantly impact your overall work environment. A question like: Where do you see yourself in five years? will help you understand what type of personality a potential hire exhibits.

Investing in Your Future

Hiring isn't just about filling a position; it's an investment in your business's and your employee's future.

Here's how to ensure a successful long-term partnership with your employee:

- **Onboarding and Training:** Provide proper onboarding and training through systems to ensure your new employees understand their role, your company culture, and your expectations.
- **Growth Opportunities:** Offer opportunities for professional development to keep your employees engaged and motivated. We pay our employees by the hour, but they receive bonuses based on different factors and their position in our company. If they are in sales, their bonus is based on the sales they produce. Technician's bonuses are based on the amount of billed hours they produce in any given week.
- **Building Trust:** Foster an environment of trust by being approachable, receptive to feedback, and open to new ideas. One question I have received a lot from handyman business owners is, "How can I trust someone to do the quality work I would do?" The short answer is: You just have to. You have to trust them because you have put them through the test. If you have done the hiring process correctly, you have identified that this person matches your core values; they talk like your core values, live your core values, and portray your core values in their work. Most people get into trouble with employees doing the wrong thing because, as a business owner, you were anxious to hire and hired the first person who applied (I say this because I have done that many times!). As handyman business owners who want to build a brand and a legacy, we need to be slow to hire and quick to fire!
- **Avoid Codependent relationships:** Codependency is something you don't hear about a lot, but it is something that I used to struggle with—and still do from time to

time. Codependency is when you find your value in how you believe others think of you. This can lead to very destructive behavior, especially with your employees, if you are not careful. If you are afraid to tell your employees the truth because they might not like what you say, then they will quickly lose trust in your leadership. For me, part of dropping my codependent behaviors was realizing that I cannot control anyone's thoughts or feelings. They are what they are, and I am who I am. The only thing I can control is my reaction to what comes about in my life. Finding healing from deep codependency has allowed me to give up control and let people be the people God created them to be and not try to force them to be the person I want them to be. Not everyone is a good fit for your business, and that is ok; you don't have to make everyone happy, that's not your job! For more info on codependency and how to overcome it, I would recommend the book "Codependent No More" by Melody Beattie.

The Hiring Mindset: A Catalyst for Growth

Shifting your mindset from solopreneur to leader lays the foundation for successful hiring and team building. By embracing collaboration and communication and focusing on cultural fit, you'll attract, retain, and empower the right employees to propel your small business forward. Remember, hiring your first employee doesn't mean losing control; it's about gaining a valuable partner in your entrepreneurial journey.

One of our business's core values is professionalism, which includes professional talk, professional dress, and professional outlook; for us, this includes punctuality and not using foul language. A few years back, we brought in a potential hire for an in-person interview. The candidate was ten minutes late for the interview, had a large gun tattooed on the inside of his right arm, and used a total of ten cuss words in the span of our 20-minute interview!

We are not discriminating; we have core values, and a specific clientele that expects a certain type of individual to show up at their home. Needless to say, we did not hire this gentleman. This is a prime example of knowing our core values and what we wanted and didn't want.

Chapter 18

Collaboration Mindset

When you are five years old and get a new soccer ball for Christmas, your tendency is to hoard it to yourself and not let others play with it. Sure, you have a lot of fun kicking that ball around the backyard by yourself, but what you don't realize is that if you brought that ball to the park and allowed others to play soccer with you, you would have exponentially more fun than you would on your own.

When we have a brand-new business that is all ours, it's hard not to want to hoard it—hoard our secrets, our successes, and our failures. When we do this, we miss out on an extraordinary opportunity. Allowing others to speak into our business can help us see the true potential, much like that five-year-old with a brand-new soccer ball!

In today's competitive landscape, collaboration can be a powerful tool for small and growing businesses. By joining forces with similar companies, you can tap into new markets, share resources, and achieve goals that might be out of reach individually. However, successful collaboration requires a specific **mindset shift** from competition to cooperation.

This chapter will guide you through cultivating the essential attitudes and practices needed to build thriving business partnerships.

Our inherent instinct might be to view similar companies as rivals. But the reality is, collaboration often leads to a win-win situation. Here's why:

- **Synergy and Shared Strength:** Combining resources, expertise, and customer bases can create a more potent force than operating independently. The thing about people is we don't know what we don't know, and what we don't know is actually a lot. One effective way to learn what we don't know is by collaborating with others on a similar path, whether they are on the same step or a few steps ahead. A valuable resource I want to recommend is the free group on Facebook called "The Handyman Journey Mastermind." This group is a wealth of knowledge and exhibits a great collaborative mentality where people help each other just for the sake of helping. Its truly fantastic!
- **Market Expansion and Access:** Partnerships open doors to new audiences and markets you might not have reached alone. Just because someone owns another handyman business in your area doesnt make them competitors. The simple truth is that they may do different handyman work than you. They may not paint and you might, and they may do plumbing and you don't. When we start thinking about how we can help others and get our minds off ourselves, we start seeing the network of potential that is in front of us!
- **Innovation and Shared Learning:** Collaboration fosters an environment for exchanging ideas and developing innovative solutions together. Again, the handyman down the street may have a time-saving way of doing gutter

cleaning that you never thought of. The most valuable people in the marketplace are the connectors; the more people you can connect, the more success you will find.

Collaboration is about putting the success of the partnership ahead of individual gains. This requires fostering a "we over me" mentality.

- **Shared Goals and Vision:** Clearly define the overall goals of the partnership and ensure both businesses are aligned for success. I cannot begin to tell you how beneficial it has been to coach and collaborate with handyman businesses all around the world. While I have helped many businesses start and grow, I have also gleaned a lot of great ideas from others who have helped my business out. I have come to really enjoy talking with other businesses; in fact, that's what I spend most of my time doing these days. I'd love the opportunity to talk with you as well. You can set up a cost-free call at www.handyman-journey.com/coaching
- **Open Communication and Transparency:** Communication is key. Share information openly, address concerns transparently, and work together to find solutions. Once you open up with others about the struggles you are having in your business, you will be surprised at how similar we all are!
- **Mutual Respect and Trust:** Each business brings value to the table. Respect each other's expertise and build trust through consistent follow-through on commitments.

A successful partnership is built on more than just the initial agreement. Here's how to cultivate a strong and lasting collaboration:

· **Clear Roles and Responsibilities:** Outline each business's roles, responsibilities, and areas of accountability to avoid confusion and ensure project progress. This may come into effect if you wish to pass work from one business to another. You and the other business owner will need to discuss factors like referral fees and customer care.

Not all collaborations are created equal. Choose your partners strategically:

· **Shared Values and Culture:** Look for businesses that align with your company values and culture. A shared foundation fosters better communication and collaboration. Ultimately you want to collaborate with businesses that share your mission and core values so that way your clients don't come back at you saying you referred them to a shock jock!
· **Complementary Strengths and Resources:** Identify partners who possess the skills or resources you lack to create a well-rounded team with a wider range of offerings.
· **Long-Term Vision:** Seek partners who share your vision for the future and are committed to the partnership's long-term success. You want to collaborate with others who you know have your best interests in mind and will treat your clients the way you would.

Shifting your mindset from "going it alone" to embracing collaboration is a powerful step towards business growth. By developing the right attitude, choosing the right partners, and fostering strong communication, you can create successful collaborations that propel your business forward and foster mutual success in a competitive marketplace. Remember, collaboration is not a zero-sum game; it's about working together to achieve bigger and better outcomes for everyone involved.

Chapter 19

Company Culture

One of the biggest excuses I hear from handymen about being reluctant to hire new employees is that they are unsure of the employee's ability to perform the job as competently as they can. It is a common concern, and you are not alone in thinking this way.

However, building a good company culture is key to ensuring that your employees deliver quality work. If done right, they will eventually deliver better work than you ever did. Building a good company culture requires work, this is ultimately working on your business, not in it. This can seem like a foreign thought to most solo guys out there, but it's the shift that needs to be taken to grow your business. Spend more time working on your business than in it.

In this chapter we will discuss the first step in making that happen: Creating and living a company culture! A positive company culture creates an atmosphere of trust, respect, and shared purpose that fosters employee engagement, productivity, and well-being.

Ultimately, business is not about the work that needs to be done, but how the work is done! The best thing we can get is a happy customer who tells more happy customers. So, how do we create a business that produces happy customers, even when we aren't there? The answer is company culture, and that all starts with core values and a mission statement.

Here's what we need to do first:

- Define your company's Core Values: What principles guide your decision-making and interactions? What are you known for in your community, or do you want to be known for?
- Articulate a meaningful mission statement: What drives you beyond generating profits? Having a mission employees can connect with creates enthusiasm and commitment.

Chapter 20

Core Values

When I was growing up, my mom was one of those moms who always had all kinds of cookies and snacks on the counter. As a child, this was my paradise! I remember many times waking up in the middle of the night, sneaking into the kitchen to grab a chocolate chip cookie and go back to bed.

Once, I even woke up in the morning with a half-eaten cookie on my pillow, and I had no clue how it had gotten there; apparently, I was a sleepwalking cookie eater! While this was any kid's dream, it has come at a cost, to make a long story short, I now need some dental work.

Recently, I reached out to a new dentist and scheduled my first check-up. When I arrived at my first appointment, I was blown away. When the dental assistant brought me to the back for my appointment, she informed me that there was a gift on the dental chair for me. Sitting on the chair was a gift bag and a card with my name on it.

I opened the card, and there was a handwritten note from the dentist. Inside the gift bag was some cool swag—well, as cool as dental swag can be. One thing that still stands out from my trip to the dentist is the insulated water cup they gave me. It had their business information on it, and my wife uses that cup almost every day. I was astonished that the dentist had given me a gift on my first visit. I sat down and settled in, just then the dental assistant came in to take X-rays of my teeth. During the five minutes it took, she talked with me to get to know me. I told her I had three kids, and have been married since 2012.

When the dentist came in, I was amazed when the dental assistant introduced the dentist to me. She told him what I did for a living, how many kids I had, and how long I had been married. I was already blown away by my experience when another lady came in who was in charge of the financial department. The dentist introduced me to her in the same manner that the dental assistant had introduced me earlier! I was impressed with the level of care and interest each person showed to me during my visit.

Then it dawned on me that these were the company's core values in action. This is a beautiful example of the power of strong core values and systems that portray those core values to the business's clients. This particular dentist has core values listed on their website, and the very first thing you see are the words "Guests are family." This is their main core value, and it is exactly what I felt during my first visit. This is how core values work when they are implemented well!

Core values will also help you hold your employees accountable and give you a clear line in the sand on whether to keep an employee or not. Employees will fit your core values or they won't; it doesn't matter how skilled they are. There is a big difference between skills and personality. Hire for personality, not skill.

Core values are the words that define you as a person and, ultimately, your business as an entity. Your core values will help guide your decision-making and business moves going forward.

Here is a list of our business's core values listed as standards of operations; these are the attributes that set us apart from other similar businesses:

Standards of Operation:

- **Communication**: Communication is key. Err on the side of over-communication. This is shown by calling/texting clients with updates and calling/texting team members with updates. Be the last to respond so people know they are heard.
- **Timeliness**: *(If you're on time, you're late; if you're early, you're on time.)* If we are running behind, we strive to let the customer know we are running late and give them an approximate ETA. Notify the customer at least 30 minutes before the scheduled appointment time.
- **Orderliness**: Have what we need when we need it.
- **Honesty**: Our pledge is to be honest about all things. This includes being honest about and presenting quicker, more cost-effective solutions to the customer's issues.
- **Integrity**: We are who we are and do the right thing even when no one is watching.
- **Initiation**: We take charge and get what needs to be done, done.
- **True to our word**: If we say we are going to do something, we do it, even if it means losing money.
- **Code followers**: While others may cut corners to save time or cost, we stick by the building codes to the best of our knowledge.
- **Respect**: We show respect to co-workers and customers at all times, even when we disagree. The customer may not always be right, but we always treat them as if they were. *(respect customer's time, their home, their family, and their opinions)*

- **Cleanliness**: We strive to leave the job site cleaner than when we arrived. Having the proper clean up tools (broom, vacuum, rags, etc.) is essential.
- **Ability**: We are honest about our abilities. If we do not feel comfortable about completing a job, we are upfront with the customer.
- **Professionalism**: We strive to look and talk in a professional manner at all times. This includes wearing the provided Honest Lee Handyman Services uniform, which consists of clean, dark blue button-up uniform shirts, having an orderly service truck, using appropriate language around customers (no profanity), and not smoking on or around the job site.
- **Team Players**: We understand that we all have different strengths and weaknesses, and we reach out to others in times of need. *(True wisdom is not having all the answers but knowing where to find the answers.)*

Core values need to be the things you do not waiver on. They are your set of principles that you live and die on. Here are some great tips to help you create your own core values:

- **Get input from everyone involved** (not just you)
- **Keep it short and sweet**: Aim for about five, one-word core values.
- **Make it specific**: Avoid vague terms like "Excellence" or "Innovation."
- **Focus on behaviors**: These should not be a stretch but actually how you act (integrity).
- **Live your values**: If you don't live them, no one will.

Chapter 21

Mission Statement

A mission statement is your company's *why* in a single sentence. This simple statement will help you and your future employees stay the course of what drives your business beyond just profits. With a clear and distinct mission statement, your employees can steer the business in the direction you would—without you being there. A strong mission statement also helps to create a sense of unity and trust between you and your employees, ensuring that they will treat your clients with respect and professionalism, even when you're not around.

Here are some great examples of iconic mission statements:

Nike: "To bring inspiration and innovation to every athlete in the world. If you have a body, you are an athlete."

Google: "To organize the world's information and make it universally accessible and useful."

Amazon: "We strive to offer our customers the lowest possible prices, the best available selection, and the utmost convenience."

Coca-Cola: "The Coca-Cola Company exists to benefit and refresh everyone who is touched by our business."

Here is our personal handyman business's mission statement that defines us as a business:

"Honest Lee Handyman Services exists to bring hope—hope for a better service, a better experience, and a better community for the reinvigoration of moral fortitude."

Our much longer business mission description goes a little more in-depth in how we do these things:

"Honest Lee Handyman Service, LLC is a company that aspires to bring hope to homeowners and businesses by helping them accomplish their repairs in a timely and efficient manner. We strive to create a one-of-a-kind experience for both our customers and our employees through teamwork, communication, and passion for the work that we do. We pride ourselves in our top-of-the-line service by being hard-working, honest, and caring for our clients every step of the way. We are committed to creating a better community by helping those who do not have a voice in their circumstances. Honest Lee Handyman Service, LLC donates 10% of our profits to help free kids out of the sex trade industry. We also donate a portion of our proceeds to help rebuild homes damaged by California wildfires. We believe in doing what is right simply because it is the right thing to do!"

When you know a business and read its mission statement, the words that come to mind should be, "Of course, that's who they are!" A properly made mission statement defines the company's purpose for existence and is useful for staying on course to the original reason why the business was created!

Here are some great tips to help you create your mission statement:

- **Define your purpose:** What is your company's reason for existence? What problem are you solving, and what impact are you looking to make?
- **Focus on the "who" and the "how":** Describe "who" you serve and how you will bring value to them.

· Keep it concise and memorable: Aim for less than 100 words and something that will stick in people's minds.
· Use strong words: Words such as "empower" and "transform" add power to your mission.
· Think Future-proof: Ensure your mission has room to accommodate future growth.

Chapter 22

Creating and Sustaining Company Culture

Your core values and mission statement are very helpful, even when you are the only one in your business. When these come into play in a big way is when you start growing your business with employees. You can have plenty of work, good pay, and even benefits, but if your business lacks company culture, no one will want to work for you for very long.

In 2018, Glassdoor, a website where employees anonymously review companies and share salary information, performed a multi-county survey that reported that over half (around 56%) of employee's value culture more for job satisfaction than salary.

Through years of managing employees and talking with thousands of growing handyman businesses, I have developed some tips for creating and maintaining a positive company culture.

Here are some key factors to focus on when building and maintaining culture in your business:

Trust and Communication:

- **Open & Honest Communication:** Encourage transparency in leadership and create a safe space for employees to voice concerns and ideas. This fosters trust and collaboration. (team players)
- **Empowerment & Autonomy:** Trust your employees to make decisions and own their work. This increases engagement and creates a sense of ownership.
- **Respect & Recognition:** Treat everyone with respect, regardless of their position in your company. Celebrate achievements and contributions to make employees feel valued.
- Recognize that others may have better ideas than you.
- Allow your employees to make mistakes and learn from them. You will quickly learn if a person is a good fit by how they react to a mistake they made.
- **Give bonuses:** Periodically read out loud reviews and reward employees with a $100 bill.
- **Set up a review reward program:** If the employee is mentioned by name, they get a $10 gift card.
- Keep a calendar of all birthdays and anniversaries and celebrate them. Have employees fill out "Favorite things" paper when they are first hired. This form will help you honor them in a way they appreciate when it is their birthday or work anniversary.

Favorite Things

Name:_____ Birthdate:_____

Cake:_____ Cookie:_____

Ice cream:_____ Dessert:_____

Restaurant:_____ Store:_____

Activity:_____ Color:_____

Hobby:_____ Gift Card:_____

Candy:_____ Food type:_____

TVShow:_____ Animal:_____

Work-Life balance and support:

- **Promote a healthy work-life balance:** You don't want to be working all the time, so don't make your employees do that either. *(Don't ask your employees to do anything you wouldn't do)*
- **Invest in employee development:** Both personally and professionally. Care about what your employees care about. (take to home building sites, host hands-on trainings, gift an employee lessons to their hobby)
- **Create and maintain a positive work environment:** Bad employees cause more harm than you think. *One bad apple can spoil the bunch.*

Community and connection:

- **Team-building activities & social events:** Build relationships with your employees outside of work. Realize employees have lives outside of work and get to know that person.
- **Mentorship programs:** Create programs or resources in your company to connect experienced employees with new hires to promote growth and shared knowledge and expertise.
- **Recognitions & Celebrations:** Host year-end company parties, randomly bring in donuts, take the team to lunch on a whim, celebrate great months by handing out cash at the end of the day.

Remember that building a strong company culture is an ongoing process and takes time. It takes continuous effort from leadership and **employees.**

Here are some additional tips:

- Get ongoing feedback from your employees.
- Lead by example. If you're not doing it, your people will not do it.
- Celebrate small wins and milestones.
- Be patient and persistent.
- Surround yourself with people who match your culture, and you will find the right people for your company. When looking for employees, start with the communities that you are already naturally involved in such as. your local Little League, Church or neighborhood. If you have people that match your culture around you, they may know others who have similar values and may be a perfect fit for your business.

Now for some homework. You have learned how to create a thriving company culture, so it's time to put that knowledge on paper.

Fill out the following core values and mission statement papers and post them on the "Handyman Journey Mastermind" group on Facebook. Doing this will help these principles become real to you and hold you accountable. It will also encourage others to create a lasting and thriving company culture for their own business.

For those of you who need a challenge, I challenge you to take some time and effort to better yourself and your business!

Building a Brand for Your Business
Core Values

Core Value	How it will be portrayed
_____	_____
_____	_____
_____	_____
_____	_____
_____	_____
_____	_____
_____	_____
_____	_____
_____	_____

Company Mission Statement

Mission Statement (Less than 100 words)

Mission Statement Description (What you do, Why and How you do it)

Chapter 23

Conclusion

I began this book by sharing a story of when a good friend challenged my fixed and scarcity mindset regarding working out and what I thought I was capable of.

As I conclude this book, I want to point out that even though my friend called out my bad mentality, it took conscious effort for me to choose to change and ultimately adopt an abundant mindset. Just as my friend delivered some hard truths to me, this is me challenging the negative mindset in you. But now it is up to you to stay conscious of that mindset and commit to making the choice to change things for the better. **It's up to you now. Others can only encourage you so much, and then it requires action.**

I also want you to know that you will never stop struggling with a negative or scarcity mindset. It's something that will always plague you as it does me and it requires a daily choice. Even as you are reading this book, know that I am struggling with some limiting mindsets. The key to success is recognizing them and calling them out for what they are. Set up guardrails in your life to combat those negative mindsets. For me those guardrails have been focusing on constant personal development, deep engagement in church, surrounding myself with people I want to emulate, and a daily surrender of control.

You can do this! Things may seem hard right now, but there is always a way around hardship. You have what it takes to keep going, and you have more in you than you think you do! Also I want you to remember, you are not alone on this handyman journey! You can set up a free phone call with me anytime, I'd love to chat, you can do this at www.handymanjourney.com/coaching.

In life when we are struggling to make a decision we often know what we need to do, we are just afraid to do it. It's ok to be afraid but it's not ok to let that fear control you. Most of the time you know enough about something, you don't need to gather any more info, you just need to take action! Slow down, take a deep breath, you got this.

Chapter 24

Your Next Step Resources:

- If you are looking for more in-depth business coaching for your handyman business you can set up a free consultation call with me at www.handymanjourney.com/coaching
- If you need help with Handyman marketing, whether it is building a website, SEO, or advertising, visit www.handymanmarketingpros.com and see how Jason Call can help you out.
- Tune into The **Handyman Success Podcast** to hear others' stories and be inspired! You can listen to it on your favorite podcast platform!
- Follow The Handyman Journey on YouTube, Instagram, and Facebook to follow along on our Handyman Journey.

YouTube: https://www.youtube.com/channel/UCHO4Ph5ithDRTski0RA0wlw

Facebook: https://www.facebook.com/HandymanJourney/

Instagram: https://www.instagram.com/the_handyman_journey/

- Join the conversation about others handyman journey on The Handyman Journey mastermind group on facebook https://www.facebook.com/groups/955093931316242/